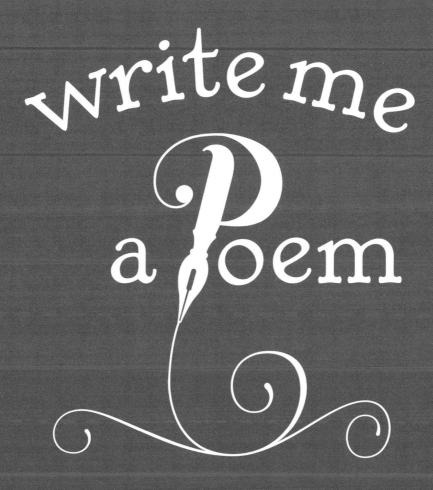

Write me a Poem

PICTURING WORDS IN A POEM

by VALERIE BODDEN
Illustrations by MONIQUE FELIX

CREATIVE EDUCATION ▪ CREATIVE PAPERBACKS

Published by Creative Education and Creative Paperbacks
P.O. Box 227, Mankato, Minnesota 56002
Creative Education and Creative Paperbacks are imprints of The Creative Company
www.thecreativecompany.us

Design and production by Chelsey Luther
Art direction by Rita Marshall
Printed in the United States of America

Photographs by Corbis (Pach Brothers), DeviantArt (Esiri76). Illustrations © by
Monique Felix. "The Red Wheelbarrow," by William Carlos Williams, from *The Collected
Poems: Volume 1, 1909–1939*, © 1938 by New Directions Publishing Corp. Reprinted by
permission of New Directions Publishing Corp.

Library of Congress Cataloging-in-Publication Data
Bodden, Valerie.
Picturing words in a poem / Valerie Bodden.
p. cm. — (Write me a poem)
Includes index.
Summary: An elementary exploration of images and personification in poetry, intro-
ducing similes, metaphors, and haiku as well as poets such as William Carlos Williams.
Includes a writing exercise.
ISBN 978-1-60818-621-1 (hardcover)
ISBN 978-1-62832-253-8 (pbk)
ISBN 978-1-56660-681-3 (eBook)
1. Poetry—Juvenile literature. 2. Personification in literature. 3. Poetry—Authorship—
Juvenile literature. 4. Poetics—Juvenile literature. I. Title.

PN1059.P47B63 2015
808.1—dc23   2015007212

CCSS: RI.1.1, 2, 3, 5, 6, 7; RI.2.1, 2, 3, 5, 6, 7; RI.3.1, 3, 5, 7; RF.1.1; RF.2.3, 4; RF.3.3

First Edition HC 9 8 7 6 5 4 3 2 1
First Edition PBK 9 8 7 6 5 4 3 2 1

Table of Contents

Word Pictures	4
All the Senses	8
It's Like …	11
It Is …	12
Becoming Human	15
Picturing Words in Haiku	16
Famous Poet: William Carlos Williams	18
Activity: Write Me a Poem	20

Glossary	22
Read More	23
Websites	23
Index	24

Word Pictures

HAVE you ever seen lights that twinkle like stars? Have you ever told your brother he's a turkey? Of course, your brother isn't a turkey. And the lights didn't look exactly like stars. We use word pictures like these to help us describe the world around us.

How would you describe fireflies at night?

POETS

use word pictures, too. These word pictures can help readers "see" the poem in their minds. Word pictures can also help the reader under-stand the poet's feelings.

A poet picks just the right words to use.

All the Senses

Readers picture a poem through images. These are words that describe things you can see, hear, smell, taste, or touch. How many images can you find in these lines from the poem "Preludes" by T. S. Eliot?

The winter evening settles down
With smell of steaks in passageways.
Six o'clock.
The burnt-out ends of smoky days.
...
The showers beat
On broken blinds and chimney-pots,
And at the corner of the street
A lonely cab-horse steams and stamps.

A prelude is something that comes before.

It's Like ...

Sometimes poets use a special type of image known as a simile (*SIM-uh-lee*). A simile uses the words "like" or "as" to compare two things. It tells the reader that one thing is "like" the other. What does this simile from the poem "Winter" by Dorothy Aldis compare?

The street cars are
Like frosted cakes—
All covered up
With cold snowflakes.

Snow can be like a blanket—or like frosting!

It Is ...

Words called **metaphors** (*MET-uh-forz*) compare two things, too. But they do not say one thing is "like" the other. Instead, they say one thing "is" the other. What are the clouds called in Christina Rossetti's poem "Clouds"?

White sheep, white sheep,
On a blue hill,
When the wind stops,
You all stand still.

What do clouds look like to you?

Becoming Human

Sometimes poets use metaphors to liken animals or objects to people. The poet talks about the objects as if they were human. This is called **personification**. What human things do the characters do in Edward Lear's poem "The Owl and the Pussycat"?

They dined on mince, and slices of quince,
Which they ate with a runcible spoon;
And hand in hand, on the edge of the sand,
They danced by the light of the moon,

Picturing Words in Haiku

Word pictures can be used in almost any kind of poem. Haiku are three-line Japanese poems. They usually do not use similes or metaphors. But they use strong images, like in this haiku by Shiki.

A mountain village
under the piled-up snow
the sound of water

Can you imagine what the village looks like?

The next time you read a poem, pay close attention to its word pictures. Soon your mind will be full of images!

Famous Poet: William Carlos Williams

AMERICAN poet

William Carlos Williams was born in 1883. He became well known for his use of images. He wrote a lot about ordinary things. Notice the images in his poem "The Red Wheelbarrow."

so much depends
upon

a red wheel
barrow

glazed with rain
water

beside the white
chickens.

Activity: Write Me a Poem

GRAB a piece of your favorite fruit.

Spend some time looking at it, smelling it, touching it, and tasting it. Now think of an image to describe the fruit. Use another image to tell what the fruit is "like." Use a third image to say the fruit "is" something else. Put your images together to make a poem.

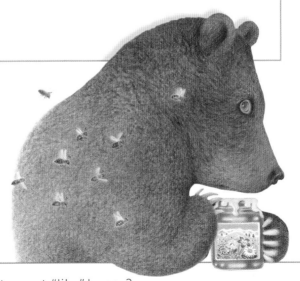

Glossary

compare	to show how two things are alike or different
describe	to use words to tell about something
images	pictures made in someone's head by words they read or hear
metaphors	words or phrases that compare two things by saying that one thing "is" the other
personification	giving human abilities or thoughts to something that is not human, like a plant or animal
simile	a word or phrase that compares two things by using the words "like" or "as"

Read More

Corbett, Pie. *Poem-maker, Word-shaker*. North Mankato, Minn.: Chrysalis, 2006.

Magee, Wes. *How to Write Poems*. Laguna Hills, Calif.: QEB, 2007.

Prelutsky, Jack. *Read a Rhyme, Write a Rhyme*. New York: Knopf, 2005.

Websites

English Club: Matching Similes Game
https://www.englishclub.com/esl-games/vocabulary/matching-similes.htm
Play this game to see how well you know some common similes.

Scholastic: Writing with Writers
http://teacher.scholastic.com/Writewit/poetry/
Listen to poets read some of their poems and check out their tips for writing poetry.

Index

Aldis, Dorothy 11

Eliot, T. S. 8

feelings 7

haiku 16

images 8, 16, 17, 19

Lear, Edward 15

metaphors 12, 16

personification 15

Rossetti, Christina 12

Shiki 16

similes 11, 16

Williams, William Carlos 19

   "The Red Wheelbarrow" 19

word pictures 4, 7, 16, 17